CODE MONKEYS
Logic

BY JOHN WOOD

BookLife
PUBLISHING

©2020
BookLife Publishing Ltd.
King's Lynn
Norfolk PE30 4LS

A catalogue record for this
book is available from the
British Library.

ISBN: 978-1-78637-978-8

Written by:
John Wood

Edited by:
Robin Twiddy

Designed by:
Danielle Webster-Jones

*All facts, statistics, web addresses
and URLs in this book were verified
as valid and accurate at time of
writing.*

*No responsibility for any changes
to external websites or references
can be accepted by either the
author or publisher.*

IMAGE CREDITS

FIRST THINGS FIRST

 **COMPUTER =** a machine that can carry out <u>instructions</u>

 **CODING =** writing a set of instructions, called code, to tell computers what to do

 **PROGRAMMER =** a person who writes code (like a human code monkey)

Computers are everywhere. Desktops, laptops, smartphones and tablets are all computers. There are even computers in surprising places, from fridges to lampposts.

Coding
IN THE WILD

All games are built out of code. It does not matter if you play games on your phone, computer or **console** – every game has been made by programmers.

The early versions of Minecraft were built by one person. Now whole teams of people work on the game.

By learning to code, you could create your own simple game one day. Games can be about anything you want – what game would you make?

Maybe you could grow up and code games all day.

WHAT IS Logic?

Computers carefully follow the programmer's code and do exactly what it says. Computers can't think for themselves — they need to be told what to do every step of the way.

This is Orangutron. She is a robot with a computer inside, and she needs to be told exactly what to do.

The order in which a computer figures out what to do is called logic. Sometimes the computer has to make a choice — this is called a decision.

The computer follows different paths in the code depending on the decisions it makes. You can think of it like the branches of a tree going in different directions.

Yes or No?

Computers can only answer simple yes or no questions. When a computer comes to a decision, it asks a question: yes or no? If the answer is yes, it follows the yes branch. If the answer is no, it follows the no branch.

It is up to the programmer to make sure the branches lead to the right places!

START HERE

Orangutron is hungry! We are going to show her how to choose a good banana. Look at the steps below. The diamond boxes mean there is a yes or no choice to make.

Pick a banana from the bunch

 Is the banana black?

YES → Too ripe! Throw that banana out of the tree!

NO

 Is the banana green?

YES → Not ripe enough! Put that banana to one side

NO

 Is the banana yellow?

YES → Perfect! Eat that lovely banana!

Using these steps, Orangutron will keep picking bananas until she has found a nice yellow one to eat.

Branching:
IF, THEN, ELSE?

In coding, **if** is used to tell the computer to make a decision. When the computer reaches an **if**, it asks if something is true or not. If the answer is yes, it follows the next instruction.

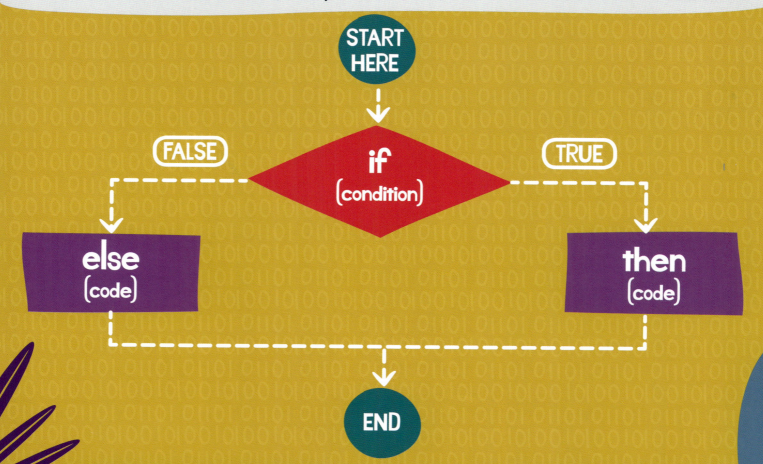

START HERE

if (condition)

FALSE

TRUE

else (code)

then (code)

END

Sometimes **if** also has an **else** part. The **else** part tells the computer what to do if the answer is no.

BABY MONKEY
if Mum is nearby → Climb on her back!
else → Look for Mum!

MORE BRANCHING: Numbers!

Computers can also **compare** numbers when asking their yes or no questions. They use maths **symbols** to ask questions. Here are a few maths symbols that are used.

== Means equal, or the same

< Means less than

> Means more than

Computers are good at maths. Let's look at an example on the next page to see some symbols in action!

Orangutron is looking after five code monkeys. Her code tells her to check if the number of monkeys is less than five (<5). If there are less than five, it means some are missing!

number of code monkeys == 5
if number of code monkeys <5 ➔ They are not all there!
Go find the missing code monkeys, Orangutron!

And, Or, Not?

Sometimes the computer checks two things before it decides yes or no. There are three ways that a computer can check more than one thing.

And

The computer checks whether two things are both yes. For example, Orangutron might ask

if monkeys are safe **and** it is night-time ⟶ Go to sleep

Orangutron will only go to sleep if BOTH of these things are true.

Or

The computer checks whether just one thing is a yes. For example, Orangutron might ask **if** there is a code monkey **or** there is a human → Say hello!
Orangutron will say hello even if only one of these things is true.

Hello!

Not

The computer checks whether something is a no. For example, Orangutron might ask **if** there is **not** food for the code monkeys →Find food
Orangutron will only follow the instructions if the answer is no.

LOOPS

Sometimes, programmers use loops. A loop makes the computer repeat every action inside that step. This saves the programmer time – instead of writing out the instructions over and over again, they can just put it in a loop.

Computers can be told to loop instructions until a certain thing happens. Here is an example.

loop until not hungry anymore
> Pick banana
> Peel banana
> Eat banana
> Check if still hungry

This loop will make Orangutron eat bananas until she is not hungry anymore. Then she will stop eating bananas.

Monkey See

Look at all this clever code that the code monkeys have been writing. This is what real code looks like.

This is **Scratch** code.

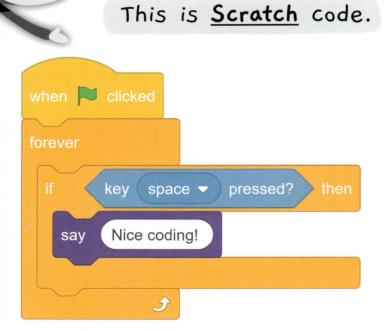

Nice coding!

The computer asks **if** the space key is pressed down. If the answer is yes, then the cat says 'Nice coding!'. If the answer is no, the cat doesn't do anything.

This is **JavaScript** code.

```
(!DOCTYPE html)
(html)
(head)
     (script)
     function getAnswer() {
     var monkey = document.getElementById("monkeyAnswer").value;
     if(monkey == "yes") { alert("Good code monkeys"); }
     if(monkey == "no") { alert("Bad code monkeys"); }
     }
     (/script)
(/head)
(body)
     (p) Have the code monkeys been good?
     (input id="monkeyAnswer" type="text"/)
     (input id="button" type="button" value="Click to submit your answer!"
onclick="getAnswer()"/)(/p)
(/body)
(/html)
```

The computer asks **if** the monkeys have been good. If 'yes', it says 'Good code monkeys'. If 'no', it says 'Bad code monkeys'.

This is **Python** code.

```
while True:
     print ("Do the code monkeys smell?")
     answer = input()
     if answer == "yes":
          print("Orangutron! Wash the code monkeys!")
     if answer == "no":
          print("Code monkeys! Go outside and play!")
```

The computer asks **if** the monkeys smell. If 'yes', it tells Orangutron to wash them. If 'no', it tells the code monkeys to go outside and play. The 'while True:' part makes the code loop, so the computer will keep asking the question.

21

Monkey Do

It is time to write your own code in Scratch. First go to
https://scratch.mit.edu/projects/editor/?tutorial=getStarted

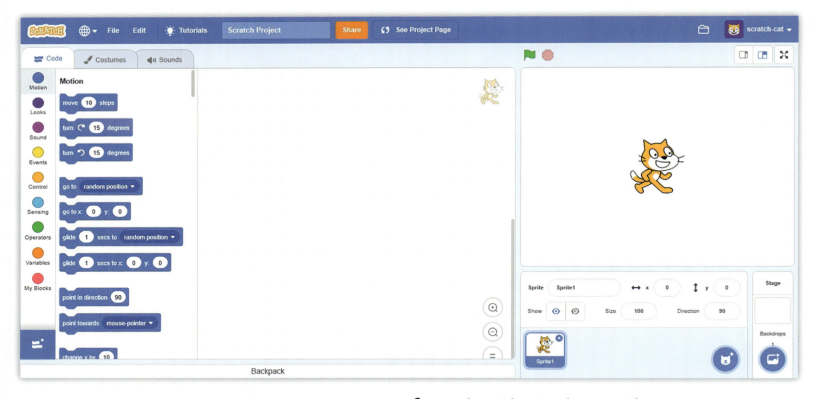

Try writing a piece of code that does this:
The cat says 'Talking about code' when the mouse is pressed down. The cat thinks 'Thinking about code' when you let go of the mouse button.

Here are the bits of code you will need. You will find them in a list on the left of the screen.

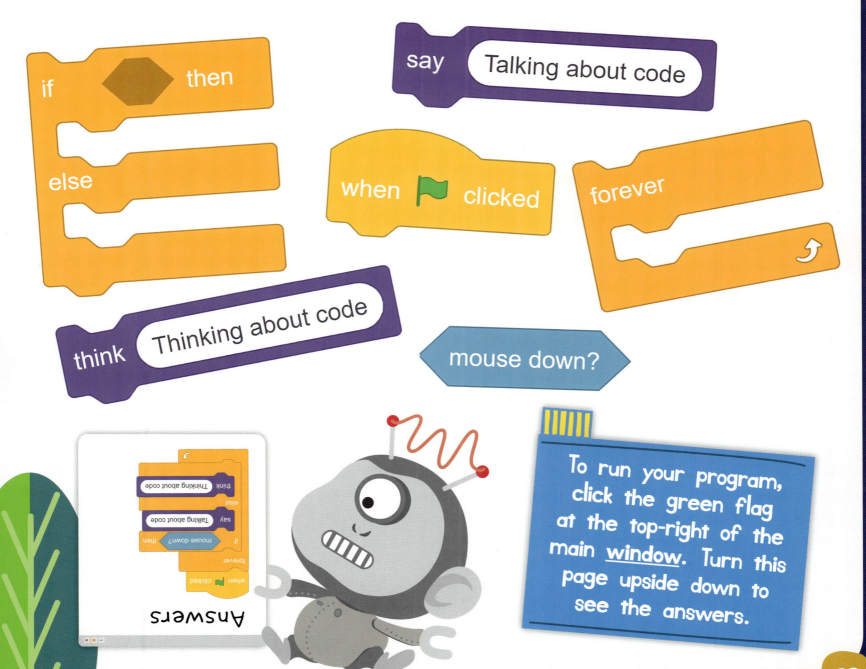

if [ ] then
else

say Talking about code

when 🚩 clicked

forever

think Thinking about code

mouse down?

Answers

To run your program, click the green flag at the top-right of the main **window**. Turn this page upside down to see the answers.

23

Glossary

compare	to look at two or more things to see what is similar or different about them
console	a computer that plays certain video games
instructions	a set of steps that explain how something is done
JavaScript	a type of programming language that is good for building websites
Python	a type of programming language that is made to be easy to use
Scratch	a type of programming language made up of pictures and words – good for learning how to code
symbols	things that are used as a sign of something else
window	(in a computer) an area of the screen where you can see a certain program running

Index